RUSSIA
UNDER THE CZARS

Read for accuracy by

Series Consultant
David McDonald
Professor of History
University of Wisconsin—Madison

A Turner Educational Services, Inc. Book based on the Turner
Broadcasting System Series "Portrait of the Soviet Union"

Library of Congress Number: 89-3686

2 3 4 5 6 7 8 9   94 93 92 91 90

Library of Congress Cataloging-in-Publication Data

Clark, James I.
  Russia under the czars / James I. Clark.
  (Portrait of the Soviet Union)
  Includes index.
  Summary: Follows the history of czarist Russia from the foundation of
the Russian state at Kiev in the mid-800s to the beginning of Romanov rule.
    1. Soviet Union—History—To 1533—Juvenile literature.   2. Soviet
Union—History—1533-1613—Juvenile literature. [1. Soviet Union—
History— To 1533.   2. Soviet Union—History—1533-1613.]   I. Title.
II. Series: Clark, James I.   Portrait of the Soviet Union.
DK71.C57   1989   947—dc19   89-3686
ISBN 0-8172-3352-0 (lib. bdg.)

Cover Photo: TBS/Reagan; Catherine the Great's palace,
                              Pushkin

RUSSIA
UNDER THE CZARS

James I. Clark

RAINTREE PUBLISHERS
Milwaukee

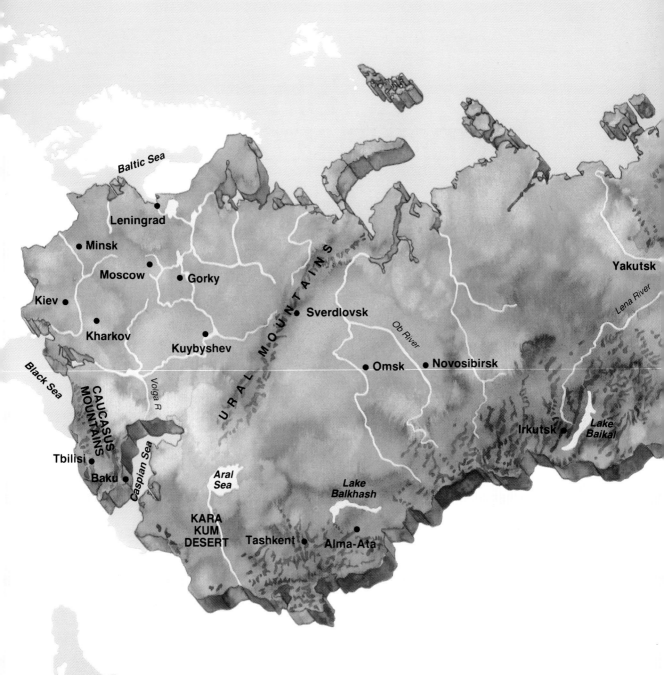

Baltic Sea

Leningrad

Minsk

Moscow

Gorky

Kiev

Kharkov

Kuybyshev

Sverdlovsk

U R A L   M O U N T A I N S

Ob River

Omsk

Novosibirsk

Yakutsk

Lena River

Black Sea

CAUCASUS
MOUNTAINS

Volga R.

Tbilisi

Baku

Caspian Sea

Aral
Sea

Irkutsk

Lake
Baikal

Lake
Balkhash

KARA
KUM
DESERT

Tashkent

Alma-Ata

CONTENTS

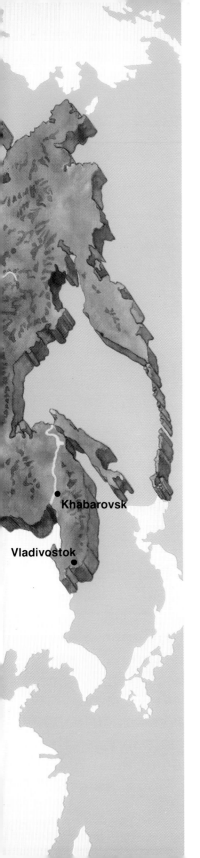

Khabarovsk

Vladivostok

INTRODUCTION

For a thousand years, what is now the world's largest country was called Russia. Then came a revolution, a change in government, a civil war, and a change in name. Russia became the Union of Soviet Socialist Republics, the U.S.S.R. Even so, many people still refer to the Union of Soviet Socialist Republics as Russia. It is also known as the Soviet Union and as Soviet Russia.

For most of those thousand years, members of two families ruled Russia. One family began with Rurik, a Viking. Descendants of Rurik led Russia until 1598. The rule of the other family began fifteen years later, with Michael Romanov. It would last until 1917.

Beginnings as a Nation

People called Slavs were among the first to live in what became Russia. Over the centuries, Slavs mixed with many different peoples, as countless armies moved into Russia from east, west, north, and south. They came to add land to empires or merely to rob, pillage, and burn. Among the invaders were Goths, Huns, Bulgars,

Leningrad became the capital of czarist Russia during the reign of Peter the Great.

Today's Soviet people are a mixture of many races and peoples. Above is a little girl from modern Soviet Georgia.

Avars, Turks, Khazars, Vikings, and Mongols. Some invaders remained only a short time. Some stayed for many years. As a result of invasions and mixtures, Russians became a blend of many peoples.

Russia's beginnings as a nation date to the 800s. By that time, such towns as Novgorod on the Volkhov River and Kiev on the Dnieper River had become great trade centers. Rivers and lakes provided easy routes between the Baltic Sea to the north and the great city of Constantinople, near the Black Sea, to the south. People wishing to trade in such goods as furs, cloth, spices, jewelry, and wine traveled those water routes. One group that did were Vikings, who came from what are now Norway, Sweden, and Denmark.

The first written record of Russian history says that in the mid-800s the Slavs of Novgorod asked the Varangian Russes, a Viking people, to rule over them and bring order to their land. Actually, the Varangian Russes may simply have taken over, uninvited. In any case, Rurik became Novgorod's ruler.

Rurik ruled an area called "the land of the Rus." And from that may have come the word Russia. No one knows for certain. The term may have come instead from the Ruhks, a people who lived in the Black Sea region.

Under Igor, Rurik's son, Kiev

Rulers of Czarist Russia

RULER	REIGN	RULER	REIGN
Ivan IV	1547-1584	Peter II	1727-1730
Theodore I	1584-1598	Anne	1730-1740
Boris Godunov	1598-1605	Ivan VI	1740-1741
Theodore II	1605	Elizabeth	1741-1762
False Dmitri	1605-1606	Peter III	1762
Basil Shuisky	1606-1610	Catherine II	1762-1796
Michael Romanov	1613-1645	Paul	1796-1801
Alexis	1645-1676	Alexander I	1801-1825
Theodore III	1676-1682	Nicholas I	1825-1855
Ivan V	1682-1696	Alexander II	1855-1881
Peter I	1682-1725	Alexander III	1881-1894
Catherine I	1725-1727	Nicholas II	1894-1917

also came under Varangian Rus control. The rulers became grand princes, to mark them off from mere princes who controlled other areas. Their land was called Kievan Russia.

The first grand princes did not live easy lives. They had little to do with palaces or fine food and clothing. They were as rugged as the soldiers and army officers they commanded. Speaking of Svyatoslav, Igor's son, an old Russian book says:

> Upon his expedition, he carried with him neither wagons nor kettles and boiled no meat, but cut off small strips of horseflesh, game, or beef and ate it after roasting it on the coals. Nor did he have a tent, but he spread out a horse blanket under him and set his saddle under his head.

Russia Becomes Christian

By the time of Vladimir I, Grand Prince of Kiev, Viking influence in Russia had faded. Vladimir I himself placed his name in history by making Russia a Christian nation.

Many of Russia's neighbors had been Christian for hundreds of years before the Russians adopted that religion. At right is Dzhvar, a Georgian church built in 604 A.D. Georgia had been Christian since the fourth century.

According to tradition, Vladimir I considered several faiths before deciding which to follow. He examined Islam, the faith of Muslims; Judaism, the Jewish religion; the Roman Catholic faith; and East-

ern Orthodox, a Christian religion centered in Constantinople. He chose the last one, was baptized in that faith, and ordered his people to adopt it. Vladimir I had many churches built. It was said that four hundred were built in Kiev alone.

The Eastern Orthodox religion spread throughout Russia, where it was called the Russian Orthodox faith. And it became a vital part of Russian life. The Orthodox Church built monasteries and schools. Priests kept historical records. The church also became wealthy through the ownership of land and forests. In many ways, the Eastern Orthodox Church became as powerful in Russia as the government itself.

As Russians became Christians, they also received an alphabet on which to base a written language. Two Orthodox missionaries, Cyril and Methodius, developed the alphabet from that used by the Bulgars, a neighboring people. It is called the Cyrillic alphabet, after Cyril, and it has thirty-two letters.

Kievan Russia developed as a land of a few rich and many poor. At the top were the grand princes, princes, and boyars, who were no-bles ranking just below princes. Some members of this ruling class grew wealthy from trade. Most gained their wealth from owning land and collecting rent from those who worked the land.

Peasants—or farmers—made up most of the many poor in Russia. Some peasants owned land, and a few became well-off. The majority, however, paid rent, and once they had paid it, they had little left to show for a year's hard work. Peasants suffered from ignorance and poverty. They, and shopkeepers, craftspersons, and others outside the upper classes, enjoyed no rights, and they had no voice in their government.

Russian society was like a pyramid. The ruling class formed the slender peak. Peasants and other poor people were the broad base. Those at the top gave orders. Those at the bottom obeyed and served. This type of society would persist for centuries in Russia.

The Mongols

Although powerful rulers, grand princes of Kiev did not enjoy long periods of peace. Princes of cities warred on them and on each other. Kievan Russia also had to

Zagorsk (above) is the seat of today's Russian Orthodox Church. Orthodoxy became the state religion after Vladimir I was baptized in the faith of his bride, the sister of Byzantine emperor Basil II. A forced conversion of Vladimir's people soon followed.

Above: Suzdal, one of the walled monasteries built during a period of war between the rulers of different towns. This warfare weakened the nation and paved the way for invasion by the Mongols.

fight off invaders. Warfare gradually weakened Russia, and by the 1200s it was ripe for conquest by an especially powerful people. These were the Mongols.

The Mongols began as nomads —people who move themselves and their belongings regularly from place to place—in southern Siberia. In the 1100s, under Genghis

Khan, Mongols conquered southern Siberia and northern China. During the 1200s, they moved south into India and west into Russia and eastern Europe. Mongols were fierce warriors. They fought with bows and arrows from the backs of shaggy, sturdy ponies. They destroyed everything in their path, killing thousands of people and burning towns and cities.

After the conquest, few Mongols remained in Russia. However, Mongol influence persisted in the form of taxes, and tax collectors often were Russians, who saw no choice but to aid their masters. For if taxes were not paid to Mongols, hordes of them would return, and thousands of Russians would pay with their lives as a result.

The city of Moscow, northeast of Kiev, had begun tax collection in the late 1100s, and the princes of Moscow proved to be good tax collectors for the Mongols. They also were clever at hiding some of the money, which they used for their own benefit.

In 1462, Ivan III, a descendant of Rurik, became ruler of Moscovy, as the area around Moscow was called. He set off on conquests of his own.

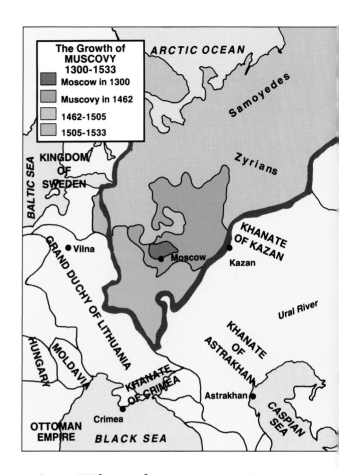

Ivan III brought numerous Russian cities under his rule. He also gained land by warring on Poland and other lands to the west. During his time, Moscow became Russia's most important city. And by the time of Ivan III's reign, the Mongols no longer enjoyed great power in Russia. Ivan III quit collecting taxes for them. A Mongol army sent toward Moscow turned back. Russia's long period under Mongol rule was over.

A Czar Called Terrible

While Ivan III called himself czar—meaning emperor—his grandson Ivan IV was the first to be crowned czar, in 1547. The czar was called "autocrat of all the Russias," a supreme ruler, blessed by the Russian Orthodox Church and by God.

Ivan IV ruled longer than any other czar in Russian history, a total of thirty-seven years. During his reign Russians expanded their territory into Siberia. They conquered land along the Volga River, and Moscow became Russia's capital.

Russia became a greater nation under Ivan IV, but he is best remembered as Ivan the Terrible, because of his cruelty, suspicions, and fits of rage. In one wild rage, he struck and killed his oldest son. Ivan IV hated boyars, and with good reason. His parents died when he was young, and boyars in the palace kept him practically a prisoner. They ruled Russia. Once he became czar, Ivan IV struck back. He had hundreds of boyars killed, along with many other enemies, real and imagined. He took over boyars' land and handed it out to men called the "serving nobility," who were loyal to him. Ivan IV also set up a secret police force to make sure his subjects remained loyal and obedient

At left is Ivan the Terrible. St. Basil's Cathedral (right) was built during Ivan's rule. After the church's completion, Ivan had its architect blinded so that no church more beautiful could be built.

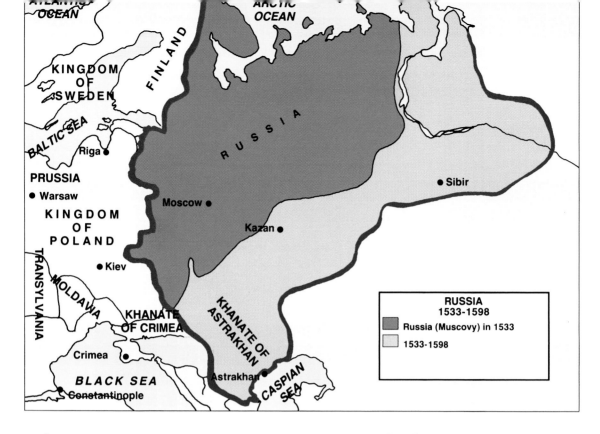

to him.

As Ivan IV gave land to the serving nobility, he also gave its members a way to be sure there were farmers to work the land for them. In the past, though poor, peasants were free to move to new land if they wished. Ivan IV made a law that put an end to this for many peasants. They became serfs, people who must remain on the land on which they were born. If the land was sold, the serfs were sold with it. Serfdom began in a small way under Ivan IV. Over the years, it grew to include millions of people. Serfs replaced free peasants as the base of the Russian pyramid.

After Ivan IV died in 1584, Russia fell into the Time of Troubles. Theodore, son of Ivan IV, was czar for fourteen years. But his wife's brother, Boris Godunov, was Russia's real ruler. Armies from Poland and Lithuania invaded the land. Russians fought Russians in civil war. Finally, a group of landowners, nobles, and others got together in 1613 to choose a czar. They selected sixteen-year-old Michael Romanov. Romanovs would rule Russia for the next three hundred years.

A Czar Called Great

During the 1700s, two Romanov czars stood out. Both are called "the Great." One was Peter I. The other was Catherine II.

Ivan IV reigned the longest as czar. Peter the Great was the tallest czar. He was six feet, eight inches tall. A visitor at the palace noted Peter's height, and went on to say that the czar was "rather thin, his face somewhat round, a high forehead, good eyebrows, a

Peter the Great sought to modernize Russia.

rather short nose, but not too short, and large at the end, rather thick lips, complexion reddish brown, good black eyes, large, bright, piercing, and well open; his look majestic and gracious when he liked, but otherwise severe and stern."

Peter became czar when he was ten years old, but he did not rule alone. He had to share the throne with his weak-minded brother, Ivan V. Peter's half-sister Sophia was the real ruler, and she remained so until 1689. In 1696 Peter alone became czar.

As a youth, Peter showed great curiosity and a desire to develop skills. He taught himself arithmetic and geometry. On his own, he learned to be a carpenter, a stonemason, and a printer. He learned to sail, to sail a boat against the wind, and to find his way on water by the stars. Peter also loved to play at war with young nobles and with boys he found on the streets of Moscow.

As czar, Peter I set out to make Russia more like western European countries. Along with a party of 250 people, he traveled to England, the Netherlands, Germany, and Sweden. On his journey, he

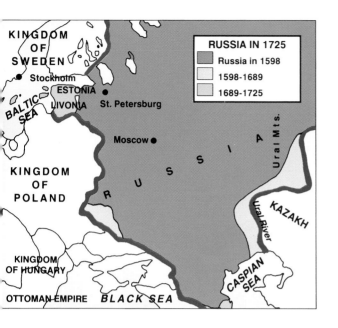

RUSSIA IN 1725

Russia in 1598
1598-1689
1689-1725

KINGDOM OF SWEDEN

Stockholm

ESTONIA

BALTIC SEA

LIVONIA

St. Petersburg

Moscow

R U S S I A

Ural Mts.

KINGDOM OF POLAND

Ural River

KAZAKH

KINGDOM OF HUNGARY

CASPIAN SEA

OTTOMAN EMPIRE   BLACK SEA

Czar Peter admired the accomplishments of the West and imported Italian architects to give his new capital a European look. The Cathedral of SS. Peter and Paul (above) boasts a 400-foot high spire.

gained information and ideas about government, organizing armies and navies, manufacturing, and transportation. He put all his new knowledge to work when he returned home.

Peter had canals built to aid transportation, and he began to build a navy, factories, and schools. He forced Russians to use the same calendar people in western Europe did, which began with the birth of Christ, instead of one that counted the years since the creation of the earth. Peter also forced Russian men to shave their beards, because beards were out of fashion in western Europe at that time. Many men objected to this, and Peter shaved some of them at court himself.

At the same time, Peter began to build a new city on the Neva River at the Baltic Sea. It became St. Petersburg, which Peter called Russia's "window to the West," and Russia's capital. Building St. Petersburg was an extremely difficult task because the land was a swamp. Thousands of workers died in the effort.

Peter the Great tried to gain land in what is now the southern Soviet Union by war with Turkey, but he

Above: *the fountains of the Petrovorets.*

failed. For twenty-one years, he fought wars with Sweden, finally winning land from that nation along the Baltic Sea. In war against Persia, he obtained land around the Caspian Sea for Russia.

Russia became a more powerful nation under Peter I, but some members of his court did not like the changes he had made. Those people believed that Alexis, Peter's only son, would take Russia back to old ways once he became czar. Peter had never thought his son tough enough to be czar. Now he began to suspect that Alexis was plotting against him, although no evidence of that was ever found. Even so, Czar Peter I had his son put in prison, and Alexis died after weeks of torture.

German-born Catherine the Great became czarina when her husband, the czar, was removed from the throne.

A Czarina Called Great

Three women were among the six rulers of Russia in the years just after Peter I's death. One was Catherine I, Peter's widow. Another was Anna, the daughter of Ivan who had shared the throne with Peter. The third was Elizabeth, Peter's daughter. The next woman on the Russian throne was Catherine II, the Great.

Catherine II had been a German princess, Sophie. When she was sixteen, she was married to Grand Duke Peter, who became Czar Peter III. Peter III was a weak man whom no one respected. With Catherine's cooperation, his enemies at court removed him from the throne shortly after he became czar in 1762. Then they murdered him. The former German princess became autocrat of all the Russias.

One observer described Catherine II as neither short nor tall, but with a majestic air. He said that she had a mixture of dignity and ease that made everyone around her comfortable. He noted, though, that "she has never been beautiful." He also noted that the czarina spoke Russian and French as well as German.

Russians had long looked upon the czar as their "little father." Now they referred to Catherine II as their "little mother."

Under Catherine II, Russia became an even larger nation. As a result of war, it took over much of Poland, what is now the Crimea region in the south, and land along the Black Sea. Catherine II encouraged scientists and writers of western Europe to visit Russia to share ideas. She had the first school for girls built in St. Petersburg, along with other schools

Above is an example of the ornate style popular during Catherine's reign. This doorway is in Catherine's Chapel.

and an art museum as well.

On the other hand, Catherine the Great also changed millions of peasants into serfs. She gave serfs to favorite generals and nobles. One general, for example,

received five thousand as a reward for winning victories over Turkey. Owners of serfs used them not

only as farmers. They also kept them as tailors, carpenters, musicians, and even as ballet dancers. One lady noble kept her hairdresser-serf in a cage so he could not tell anyone that she really was bald and wore a wig.

During the reign of Catherine II, a man named Emelyan Pugachev led serfs and peasants in revolt. Her army put down the revolt and many of those who took part were hanged. Pugachev himself was brought to Moscow in a cage. There he was put to death.

Above: the enameled domes of Catherine's Palace at Pushkin. The interior at left mirrors the czarina's taste for European manners and style. During her reign French became the language of the court.

Forced to withdraw from a burning Moscow, Napoleon's army was pared to one-twentieth of its original size by the long retreat through a Russian winter.

War with France

Paul, son of Catherine, followed her to the throne. He had reigned only five years when assassins broke into his bedroom one night and murdered him. His son became Czar Alexander I.

During Paul's short reign, in the late 1790s, Napoleon Bonaparte became ruler of France. He set out to conquer all of Europe, and England as well. After becoming czar, Alexander I at times favored England. At other times, he supported France. But after Napoleon had conquered Italy, Spain, and Ger-

many, he came to believe that the French would now invade Russia. Alexander I was right.

Napoleon and his army of 600,000 began the invasion of Russia in the summer of 1812. Russian armies retreated deeper and deeper into that vast country. As winter came on, the French reached Moscow, only to have the Russians burn the city. This left Napoleon's Grand Army without shelter or supplies, and Napoleon and his men began a long retreat toward the west. Russian armies now attacked. And of the 600,000

Frenchmen who had marched into Russia, only about 30,000 escaped death from Russian soldiers, starvation, or the bitter cold of winter.

Over the years, educated Russians had learned more and more about western European countries. Many of those countries were far ahead of Russia in industry, science, and technology. They had great universities. Such nations as France and England had parliaments, where elected representatives of the people met to make laws. In European countries, serfdom had long since disappeared, and in some countries, at least, citizens enjoyed rights and liberties.

In Russia, though, the czar remained an autocrat, answerable to no one. Russia did not have a constitution. It had no parliament to make laws. There were not individual rights or liberties, and the secret police kept track of thousands of persons. A great majority of Russians did not know how to read or write, and millions of Russians lived in serfdom.

Some of this changed under Alexander I. He abolished the secret police. People from foreign countries were allowed in Russia.

Except for serfs, everyone would now have the right to own land, and the czar granted freedom to a few thousand serfs. Alexander I also had a constitution written, although it never went into effect.

Alexander I died in 1825, and it was not certain who would become czar. Alexander I had no children, but he had two brothers, Constantine and Nicholas. Constantine, who lived in Poland, was the elder, but he did not want the throne. The other brother then became Nicholas I.

Some years before that, numerous young nobles and army officers had been meeting secretly to discuss further changes in Russia.

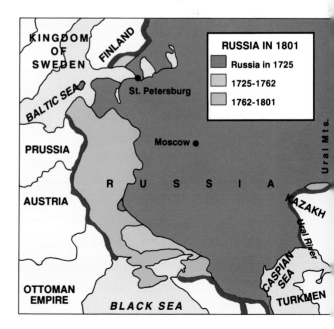

Among other things, they wanted Russia to have a constitution and rule by law instead of by a small upper class. They also wished Constantine to be czar.

They thought of themselves as revolutionaries, people who wanted to bring great and lasting change. In the past, in Russia, there had been numerous peasant and serf rebellions. These destroyed lives and property, and were brutally put down. There had been revolts in the palace, aimed only at replacing one czar with another. Some had succeeded; others had not. But the aims of the young army officers and nobles were different. They wanted to begin to change Russian society entirely. And they wished to do so in the name of ideals and progress.

In December 1825, thousands of army officers and some soldiers gathered in St. Petersburg. They were there to demonstrate for change. Nicholas I had guns and cannons turned on them. Later he had some of the demonstrators hanged. He sent others to labor camps in Siberia. The so-called Decembrist Revolt ended in failure.

Nicholas I now placed universities under police supervision. He would not allow Russians to travel outside the country. He forbade public meetings. The secret police sought out anyone who might cause the slightest trouble to the czar and his government and especially those suspected of being revolutionaries.

Under Nicholas I, Russia gained more land along the Black Sea at the expense of Turkey. Russia then came into conflict with England and France, along with Turkey, in the Crimean War, in 1853. Russia lost, and it had to give up land it had taken from Turkey.

Change Under Alexander II

Alexander II became czar upon the death of Nicholas I in 1855. He was a czar who seemed to believe in change, although it did not go as far as many Russians thought it should.

Villages and towns received the right to govern themselves through elected representatives under Alexander II. He granted Russians the right of trial by jury. He allowed newspapers some freedom to decide what to print. He set up a system of banks and encouraged the building of railroads. Alexander II also freed the serfs.

Czar Alexander II was killed by assassins.

Some fifty million serfs gained freedom in 1861. They were also to have the right to buy land that landowners were ordered to turn over to the government.

For the most part, landowners let go of only their poorest land. And most of the land was bought by communes—groups of families—not by individuals. Many Russian farmers did not like the idea of ownership by communes. They wanted individual, private ownerships.

Several million of the fifty million serfs had worked in their masters' homes. They knew nothing about farming. They were freed, but nothing more. Many had to move to cities, where they found jobs only at low wages, if at all.

Although cities were growing in population, four out of every five Russians lived in rural areas. About half the land was farmed for the government by what were called state peasants. State peasants turned over most of their crops to the government, which then sold them to gain income.

Russia remained a backward nation compared to many others. But during the 1800s, it made progress. Along with the changes Alexander II brought about, more and more factories were built to turn out clothing, shoes, machinery, and iron and steel. Shipbuilding had become an important industry. Thousands of miles of railroads were built. The greatest of them all, the Trans-Siberian, ran about 5,000 miles (8,000 kilometers) from Moscow to Vladivostok on the Pacific Ocean. That railroad did much to help develop the vast natural resources of Siberia. Perhaps, had Russia become

Nicholas II was the last czar to rule the Russians. He and his family ended their lives in a basement room, shot to death by the Red Army.

more of an industrial nation, peaceful instead of bloody change might come to Russian society. But this was not to be.

More and more people in Russia came to believe that change did not come quickly enough or go deeply enough. The spirit of revolution grew. One group of revolutionaries, called "The People's Will," concluded that the only way to bring about real and lasting change was to kill the czar.

Members of The People's Will tried seven times to murder Alexander II. Finally, in 1881, they succeeded. As the czar rode in a carriage in St. Petersburg, a revolutionary threw a bomb. It killed the horses and one of Alexander's officers. Police seized the bomb-thrower, and Alexander got out of his carriage. He thanked God that he had escaped. "It's too early to thank God!" another revolutionary shouted. He threw a second bomb. That one blew off Alexander's legs, and he died within hours.

Alexander's son became Czar Alexander III. He clamped down on freedoms, and gave nobles even more power over peasants and other lower classes. He also reduced the power of town and village governments. Alexander III's secret police were especially hard on anyone suspected of being a revolutionary. The population of prisoners in Siberia grew.

Nicholas II Takes the Throne

Nicholas II became autocrat of all the Russias in 1894. He was a gentle, handsome man, and a considerate and loving husband and father. He had married a German princess, Alix, who took the name Alexandra. They had four daughters—Anastasia, Tatyana, Olga, and Marie—and a son, Alexis. Nicholas II was not a strong personality, and he preferred tennis, hunting, and swimming to attending to the duties of government. Nicholas II hated conflict and argument, and he willingly let his wife make family decisions and even decisions about government. Nicholas II was not the right person to be czar during the troubled times that lay ahead, when Russia badly needed strong and thoughtful leadership.

Alexandra and Nicholas II were overjoyed on June 30, 1904, when their son Alexis was born. Now there was a male heir to the throne. But, unfortunately, Alexis suffered from hemophilia, a disease that prevents the blood from clotting. Bruises and internal injuries were especially threatening. Alexis would have to lead a careful, sheltered life.

The illness of the young heir Alexis made the royal family vulnerable to the influence of the faith-healer Rasputin.

About a year after Alexis was born, there appeared at the palace a strange, bearded holy man named Grigori Efimovich Norykh. He had been born in the village of Pokrovshoe in Siberia. His nickname was "Rasputin," which may have meant "crossroads," from the fact that several roads met and crossed in his native village. Rasputin's outstanding feature was his piercing eyes—he seemed able to hypnotize a person with them. He also seemed to have a gift of prophesy and of healing.

Rasputin won favor with Alexandra because he was able to help Alexis. He could cure the boy's headaches, sometimes by only talking to him on the telephone. Whenever Alexis was frightened or upset, Rasputin could easily sooth him. No one, doctors included, understood how Rasputin accomplished what he did.

Perhaps it was psychosomatic. That is, Rasputin made Alexis believe that the bleeding and the headaches would stop, and they did. Or perhaps it was hypnosis. No one knows.

To Alexandra, Rasputin seemed a miracle-worker. She referred to him as "our friend," who has been "sent to us by God."

The holy man's influence at the palace grew. Eventually he was making decisions that had to do with government, for example, decisions on who should be removed from or appointed to which office. Rasputin also gained a reputation for wild carousing and heavy drinking. Members of the court grew to fear him. Some leaders of the Orthodox Church denounced him as a creature of the Devil. But to Alexandra, and as a result to Nicholas II, Rasputin could do no wrong. His great influence on the royal family persisted for many years.

War in the East and Bloody Sunday

Russians got a male heir to the throne in 1904. They also went to war with Japan. Many people welcomed both, and advisors to Nicholas II believed that "a small, victorious war" might take people's minds off discontent, bolster loyalty to the czar, and remove any need for drastic change in the country. The war turned out to be small, and short, but it was far from victorious for Russia.

Russia wanted to build its influence in China and Korea. It wanted trade and raw materials for manufacturing. The Japanese government was also interested in China and Korea, and Russian activities there angered it. When it looked as though Russia might try to take over Korea, Japan struck. Without warning, its ships attacked Russian ships in the area. Then Japan declared war.

Only about fifty thousand Russian troops were stationed in the Far East. Japan had hundreds of thousands nearby. Russia had to depend on the Trans-Siberian Rail-

War in the Far East meant Russia had to rely on the narrow artery of the Trans-Siberian Railroad to move supplies. Below: Russian soldiers repair track. Right: a postcard shows Japan's modern army.

road to send more troops, as well as supplies, 5,000 miles (8,000 km.) to the scene of action. Japan, much closer to the fighting, could easily supply its armies.

Japan won victories on land. Ships of the Russian navy sailed more than halfway around the globe to attack the Japanese fleet. Russian warships set out from the Baltic Sea, moved through the Mediterranean Sea, and around Africa east to the China Sea. There the Japanese fleet awaited them, and in May 1905 the Japanese blew the Russian ships out of the water. Russia accepted defeat. The war was over.

Defeat at the hands of such a small country as Japan shamed and angered Russians. They blamed their government and their czar. Demands for representative government and other changes now grew louder. Nicholas II did not respond.

In addition to defeat in 1905, Russians had other troubles that year. Harvests in 1904 had been bad. Thousands of peasants faced starvation. As winter neared, city people also felt the pinch of food

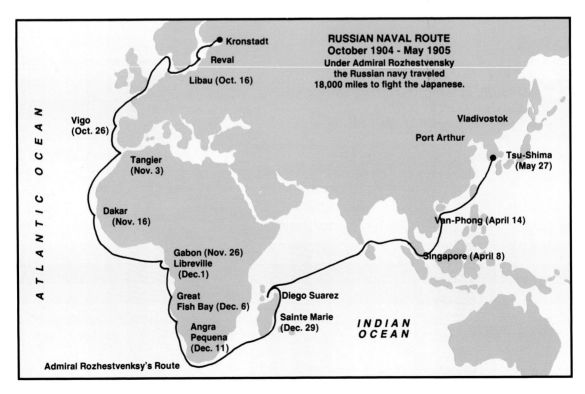

RUSSIAN NAVAL ROUTE
October 1904 - May 1905
Under Admiral Rozhestvensky
the Russian navy traveled
18,000 miles to fight the Japanese.

Kronstadt

Reval

Libau (Oct. 16)

Vigo (Oct. 26)

Vladivostok

Port Arthur

Tangier (Nov. 3)

Tsu-Shima (May 27)

Dakar (Nov. 16)

Van-Phong (April 14)

Gabon (Nov. 26)
Libreville (Dec.1)

Singapore (April 8)

Great Fish Bay (Dec. 6)

Diego Suarez

Sainte Marie (Dec. 29)

INDIAN OCEAN

Angra Pequena (Dec. 11)

ATLANTIC OCEAN

Admiral Rozhestvenksy's Route

Having emerged from isolation only forty years earlier, Japan won standing as a world power by its 1905 victory over Russia. The war's end was celebrated with victory parades in Tokyo (above) and Yokohama (right).

scarcity.

Workers in St. Petersburg began to organize for action. Steelworkers went on strike when news of Russia's defeat in war arrived, and soon workers in other factories joined them. The secret police planted a spy, George Gapon, among the workers to try to influence them against drastic action. Gapon, however, came to sympathize with the workers.

The "little father" was not in St. Petersburg. He was at his country palace. Troops on foot and on

On "Bloody Sunday" troops fired into a crowd marching on the Winter Palace to petition the czar. Two hundred were killed. At right is the Winter Palace today.

On Sunday, January 22, 1905, Gapon led some two hundred thousand workers in a march on the Winter Palace in St. Petersburg. They would present a petition to the czar, calling for a constitution, representative government, and better working conditions in factories. "O Sire," the petition read in part, "we working men of St. Petersburg, our wives and children, and our parents, have come to you, our ruler, in search of justice and protection. We are beggars, we are oppressed and overburdened with work, we are insulted, we are not looked upon as human beings but are treated as slaves."

horseback met the marchers though, and they opened fire. More than a hundred men, women, and children were killed on Bloody Sunday, and thousands were wounded. Nicholas II had not

Nicholas II created the Duma in reply to cries for reform. Above: workers occupy the assembly during the 1917 revolution.

given an order to fire, but he was blamed for the slaughter. The czar now became an object of hatred in the eyes of many Russians.

Revolution frightened Nicholas II, and he granted Russians the right to elect representatives to make laws. Together the representatives were called the Duma, which means "a group of advisors." Nothing much came of it. At its first meeting, the Duma declared that the highest authority in Russia belonged to the czar. A few laws were passed, but most Duma meetings resulted in just talk. Nicholas II could tell the members of the Duma to go home whenever he wished, which he did. In the meantime, war came to Russia once again.

World War I

There had been no great war in Europe for a hundred years, since the final defeat of Napoleon Bonaparte in the days of Czar Alexander I. But the nations had been preparing for war. They had built up their armies and navies and had made war plans. They also had made agreements as to who would help whom should war break out. Germany agreed to aid Austria-Hungary, which lay south and east of Germany. England, France, and Russia agreed to act together.

On July 28, 1914, a young revolutionary named Gavilo Princip murdered Archduke Franz Ferdinand, heir to the throne of Austria-Hungary. Princip was a citizen of Serbia, a small, nearby country. The government of Austria-Hungary believed that the Serbian govern-

Some Events During World War I

1914	
June	Archduke Ferdinand is murdered.
July	War begins.
August	Germany declares war on Russia.
	Austria-Hungary attacks Russia.
1915	
May	Germans sink the liner *Lusitania*.
August	First international Socialist conference.
1916	
April	Second Socialist conference.
December	Rasputin is murdered.
1917	
February	Widespread strikes in Petrograd.
March	Nicholas II and family are arrested.
April	United States declares war on Germany.
October	Bolsheviks take power in Russia. Lenin is dictator.
1918	
November	World War I ends.

Chart Design: Eileen Rickey

ment had been behind the killing. It demanded that Serbia do certain things within a certain time. When that country's government did not act quickly enough, Austria-Hungary declared war on Serbia. Germany supported Austria-Hungary. Russia supported Serbia. England and France supported Russia. One after another, the nations declared war.

Most soldiers in World War I wore steel helmets in battle. That gave them some protection from bullets and from deadly flying bits of steel from exploding cannon shells. Russian soldiers wore only cloth caps with visors. And that was not the only problem Russians faced in war.

Russian factories could not produce enough guns, cannons, ammunition, clothing, and other supplies and equipment the armies needed. Russian railroads could not handle the task of moving equipment and supplies to the war zones. The country had few trucks, and no paved roads. Transportation by road was mostly by horse-drawn wagon.

Russia's disastrous entry into World War I cost three-and-one-half million lives and brought czarist rule to an end.

41

Poorly equipped and badly trained, Russian troops were killed and captured by the thousands. These prisoners surrendered to the Germans in Galzia.

Soldiers often went into battle with only one rifle for every two or three or more. Without rifles, soldiers could fight only at close quarters, with bayonets, or wait until a comrade with a rifle fell dead or wounded. Still, Russians won some battles against armies of Austria-Hungary. They lost battles against Germans.

About all the country had going for it was the courage of Russian soldiers, and before the war was a year old, four million of them had been killed, wounded, or taken prisoner. To thousands of Russian soldiers, courage was one thing, but foolishness was another. As the war continued, soldiers began to desert and find their way back home.

Nicholas II made things worse by removing from office government officials who were capable. He replaced them with men who did not know what they were doing. Nicholas himself finally took over command of all the armies, even though he knew nothing about armies and war.

Many people blamed Rasputin for Nicholas' actions. This was probably right, for Rasputin influenced Alexandra, and she influenced Nicholas. Many people also believed that the holy man was giving Russian war secrets to the Germans. This was probably wrong. A group of nobles decided to kill Rasputin.

On a December night in 1916, Rasputin's murderers invited him to a party in a basement room at one of the noble's houses in St. Petersburg. They fed him poisoned wine and cakes. This hardly touched the man. Then one of the plotters shot him. They left the room thinking he was dead. But Rasputin still lived, and with a

roar, he lurched up the stairs after them. Finally, the nobles dragged him to the Neva River and dropped him from a bridge through the ice. The body was found two days later.

The End Approaches

The Russian people had been enthusiastic about war at first. Most of them disliked Germans and Germany. They cheered when the name *St. Petersburg*, a German phrase, was changed to *Petr-*

Many blamed Russia's war failures on the influence of Rasputin over the czar.

НЕГРАМОТНЫЙ тот-же СЛЕПОЙ
ВСЮДУ ЕГО ЖДУТ НЕУДАЧИ И НЕСЧАСТЬЯ·

Above: a revolutionary poster urges literacy, warning that one unable to read is like a blind man. Top of right-hand page: sailors from the crusier Aurora lend their support to the revolution. Bottom right: citizens raise barricades against government troops.

ograd, a Russian word. As the war continued, though, the Russian people grew grim, bitter, and rebellious.

In Russian cities, food became scarce, and the prices of food, fuel, clothing, and other necessities went up and up. There was plenty of food in the countryside but not enough transportation to get much of it to cities. People rioted when they could not buy even bread. Factory workers went on strike, and troops were called out to force them back to work. Defeat at the hands of Germans humiliated Russians, and there were few families that did not have a close or distant relative killed or wounded. The great majority of Russians now opposed the war, and they blamed the czar for the way the war had gone for their country.

In March 1917, change came suddenly and unexpectedly. Mobs of hungry people rioted in Petrograd. Troops were called out, but soldiers refused to act against the crowds. They joined the riot. Nicholas II ordered members of the Duma to go home. They refused. Instead, they demanded that Nicholas throw out his incompetent officials and make other changes in government. When Nicholas did nothing, members of the Duma organized their own government.

Nicholas II now knew that the end had come. The last Romanov autocrat of all the Russias abdicated. He gave up his right to the throne. Nicholas II left his army headquarters to join his family in the country. The time of Romanovs and all other czars was over.

A Chronology of the Soviet Union

800s The Viking Rurik is the first ruler of Russia. The first Russian state is established. Kiev is the center of government.

988 Vladimir I introduces Christianity to Russia. The Cryllic alphabet is adopted.

1200s Russia comes under Mongol rule.

Late 1400s Czar Ivan III ends Mongol rule.

1547 Ivan IV becomes first crowned czar.

1613 After ten years of civil war Michael Romanov becomes czar. His family will rule Russia for three hundred years.

1703 Peter I founds St. Petersburg; he tries to bring Western ways to Russia.

1812 Napoleon invades Russia with an army of 600,000 but is badly defeated.

1825 Some nobles and army officers demand rule by law. Members of this "Decembrist Revolt" are hanged by Nicholas I.

1861 Alexander II frees the serfs. Some towns gain self-government.

1905 Russo-Japanese war is fought, and Russia is defeated. Nicholas II is forced to establish representative government.

1914-1917 With France and England, Russia enters World War I against Germany and Austria-Hungary.

1917 Revolt forces Nicholas I out. Lenin becomes dictator. The Soviet Union withdraws from World War I.

1918-1921 Civil war with anti-Communists rages.

1922 The Union of Soviet Socialist Republics is established.

1924 Lenin dies, and Joseph Stalin gains power over the Communist party.

1929 Stalin becomes dictator.

1939 World War II begins in Europe.

1941 The Soviet Union enters the war on the side of the allies after being attacked by Germany.

Late 1940s In the years following World War II, the Soviet Union takes over Poland, Hungary, Yugoslavia, and other eastern countries, creating the Iron Curtain.

1953 Joseph Stalin dies and Nikita Khrushchev comes to power.

1956 Khrushchev criticizes Stalin's methods of ruling and announces the philosophy of peaceful coexistence with the West.

1957 The Soviet Union launches *Sputnik I,* the first spaceship to orbit the earth.

1960 The Soviet Union brings down a U.S. intelligence-gathering plane.

1961 Yuri Gagarin becomes the first person to orbit the earth.

1962 Soviet missile bases are discovered in Cuba, causing tension between the United States and the Soviet Union. The bases are later removed.

1964 Khrushchev is forced to retire. Leonid Brezhnev becomes head of the Communist party.

1980-1985 Four heads of government die.

1985 Mikhail Gorbachev becomes head of the Communist party. He announces great changes in the Soviet Union in the form of *glasnost* (openness) and *perestroika* (making over).

1985-1988 Gorbachev and President Ronald Reagan meet five times. The Soviet Union and the United States agree to reduce the number of their nuclear weapons.

1989 The Soviet Union withdraws its troops from Afghanistan and also agrees to cut its armed forces by 500,000.

Map of the Soviet Republics

REPUBLIC	POPULATION*	CAPITAL
Russian S.F.S.R.	144,000,000	Moscow
Ukraine	50,900,000	Kiev
Uzbekistan	18,500,000	Tashkent
Kazakhstan	16,000,000	Alma-Ata
Belorussia	10,000,000	Minsk
Azerbaijan	6,700,000	Baku
Georgia	5,270,000	Tbilisi
Tadzhikistan	4,600,000	Dushanbe
Moldavia	4,100,000	Kishinev
Kirghizia	4,000,000	Frunze
Lithuania	3,600,000	Vilnius
Armenia	3,345,000	Erevan
Turkmenistan	3,200,000	Ashkhadbad
Latvia	2,600,000	Riga
Estonia	1,542,000	Tallin

*Mid-1980s estimate

INDEX